Macbeth

WILLIAM SHAKESPEARE

● for Key Stage 3 ●

Guide written by

Ron Simpson

A *Letts* EXPLORE Lite

First published 1999
Reprinted 2000 (twice), 2001 (twice)

Letts Educational
414 Chiswick High Road
London
W4 5TF
Tel: 020 8996 3333
e-mail: mail@lettsed.co.uk

Text © Ron Simpson

Series editor Jo Kemp

Sample questions Jeff Morton

Typeset by Jordan Publishing Design

Text design Jordan Publishing Design

Cover and text illustrations Ivan Allen

Design © Letts Educational Ltd

Acknowledgements

British Library Cataloguing in Publication Data
A CIP record for this book is available from the British Library

ISBN 1 85758 862 2

Printed and bound in Great Britain by
Ashford Colour Press Ltd, Gosport, Hampshire

Letts Educational is the trading name of Letts Educational Ltd, a division of Granada Learning Ltd. Part of the Granada Media Group.

Contents

MACBETH.

MACBETH HAS TRIUMPHED IN BATTLE...

ALL HAIL, MACBETH!... THANE OF CAWDOR!... THAT SHALT BE KING HEREAFTER.

HE BADE ME CALL THEE THANE OF CAWDOR!

LADY MACBETH RECEIVES GREAT NEWS...

...SHALT BE WHAT THOU ART PROMISED.

... BUT MACBETH HAS HIS DOUBTS.

WE WILL PROCEED NO FURTH IN THIS BUSINESS.

NOT
IL.

IS THIS A
DAGGER I
SEE BEFORE
ME?

⑥

⑦

IG DUNCAN IS DEAD.

R ROYAL MASTER'S
MURDERED.

HIS SONS FLEE AND
MACBETH BECOMES KING.

I'LL TO
ENGLAND.

TO
IRELAND
I.

⑨

MACBETH PLOTS BANQUO'S MURDER,

FLY, GOOD FLEANCE!

BUT IS TORMENTED BY HIS GHOST

MACBETH TURNS TO THE WITCHES FOR GUIDANCE.

BEWARE MACDUFF!

NONE OF WOMAN BORN...

GREAT BIRNAM WOOD...

...ETH PURSUES MACDUFF,
...

...E IS YOUR HUSBAND?

HE IS IN ENGLAND, JOINING FORCES WITH MALCOLM.

(15)

...Y MACBETH GOES MAD TAKES HER LIFE.

YET HERE'S A SPOT.

MACDUFF SLAYS MACBETH AND MALCOLM IS CROWNED KING.

(18)

■ Who's who in *Macbeth*

Macbeth

The character of Macbeth dominates the play. He takes on a series of good and honourable men in turn: Duncan (Acts 1 and 2), Banquo (Act 3) and Macduff and Malcolm (Acts 4 and 5). However, his motives and character change throughout the play. At first Macbeth appears as a loyal and brave general of King Duncan, but you should notice how easily his ambition is stirred. The witches hail him as Thane of Cawdor and future king, and he begins thinking of the Crown as soon as news comes of his appointment as Thane of Cawdor. Early in the play Macbeth struggles to make a choice between ambition and honour, but honour disappears once he has killed Duncan. As he becomes more evil, he also becomes more fearful. He sees Banquo and Macduff as enemies because of the witches' (or apparitions') predictions, but Macbeth's plots are aimed at innocent children as well as the decent men he sees as a threat to his future. As Lady Macbeth becomes less powerful, Macbeth relies too much on the witches, who both confirm his fears and make him too confident about surviving: 'no man born of woman' shall kill him, and the Crown is safe until Birnam Wood comes to Dunsinane. By the end of the play Macbeth has lost much of his will to live, not even reacting to his wife's death, but at least he dies like the brave warrior he was at the start of the play.

Lady Macbeth

Lady Macbeth is described by Malcolm as a 'fiend-like queen', but she is not really a devil. Macbeth first has the idea of killing Duncan, but it is Lady Macbeth who gives it form. In Acts 1 and 2 she is in charge, organising the murder, bolstering her husband's courage, keeping up appearances with a smile or a faint.

However, there is something unnatural about this. She denies all feminine qualities in herself and thinks guilt can be washed away like a blood stain. This guilt will return to haunt her as she ends her life replaying her sins in her sleep and then committing suicide. Between her part in Duncan's murder and her final collapse she plays the part of Macbeth's queen, but she is no longer let into his secrets. For instance, in the case of Banquo's murder she is told nothing and is mainly involved in covering up Macbeth's ravings at the Ghost. She appears devilish at the beginning, but finally she is another victim of her and her husband's ambition.

Macduff

Although he is the main cause of Macbeth's downfall, Macduff takes little part in the first three acts. However, his few appearances hint at his mistrust of Macbeth, especially in his conversation with Ross and the Old Man in Act 2, Scene 4. Why should he refuse to go to Scone for the coronation unless he suspects Macbeth of evil? Although he has appeared so little in the play at that stage, it is no surprise that the First Apparition tells Macbeth to beware Macduff. He is, in many ways, the opposite of Macbeth: a loving family man, a lord whose honour is proved by his questioning of Malcolm in Act 4, Scene 3. Macduff is marked out to kill Macbeth both by the method of his birth and by his loyalty to the Royal Family. His hatred for Macbeth is increased by the horrific cruelty of the murder of his wife and family.

Banquo

In the early stages of the play Banquo has a similar role to Macduff's later on. He, too, is honourable. He appears (unlike Macbeth) as a family man and gives Macbeth no real cause for the vicious and cowardly assault he is subjected to. In an opposite situation to that of Macduff, Banquo dies and his son, Fleance, survives so that Macbeth gains nothing by his crime.

Banquo is seen by Macbeth as an enemy for two main reasons. The general reason is that his goodness and valour shame and alarm Macbeth, but the more precise motive for killing Banquo is that the Witches prophesied that his descendants would be kings of Scotland. There is no suggestion that Banquo or Fleance has any such scheme, but Banquo triumphs over Macbeth in death: Fleance lives and Banquo's Ghost unhinges Macbeth. Finally, Banquo's Ghost appears in Act 4, Scene 1, pointing at the line of future kings as his descendants.

Duncan

Duncan is the image of the good, kind, responsible old king. His few appearances show him to be decisive (the execution of Cawdor), generous and well able to balance rewards between his sons and his generals. He honours and praises Macbeth, but promotes Malcolm to Prince of Cumberland. Duncan's reputation as an almost saintly king is based as much on the words of others as on his limited appearances: you will find that even Macbeth constantly praises his goodness. Duncan's only fault, one shared by many of Macbeth's victims, is that he is too trusting.

Malcolm and Donalbain

The two sons of Duncan are shadowy figures in the first two acts of the play and Donalbain remains so, never re-appearing after his flight to Ireland. Their decision to flee Scotland (and Macbeth) is very understandable and probably wise in the long term, although it means that they are blamed at first for their father's murder. By the time that Malcolm is next seen, he is much changed. He has learned cunning, a rare quality in Macbeth's opponents: he tests Macduff's loyalty with a series of lies and comes up with the plan to conceal the numbers of his army with boughs from the trees of Birnam Wood. The action of the play must take some length of time (months? years?) and, as Macbeth declines, young Malcolm grows up, gaining a royal sense of authority.

The Witches

The Witches have magical powers and are not simply mortal women who can make predictions. Note, for instance, the way in which they disappear in Act 1, Scene 3, the supernatural adventures they describe and their ability to summon apparitions. They may also be seen in alliance with Hecate, Queen of Darkness, although there is much doubt as to whether the main Hecate scene is actually by Shakespeare. The Witches, with their colourful spells, songs and dances, and enmity towards mankind, are striking characters. However, the most important feature is their approach to Macbeth. They are waiting for him at the very beginning of the play and their two major scenes with him show them luring him into danger or confusing him by both frightening him and encouraging him. In the scene on the heath they tempt him into evil and in the apparitions scene they make his downfall certain. The Witches, like the Ancient Greek oracles, manage to deceive by telling the truth.

Nobles and lords

The lords are known as 'thanes', an old Scottish word, until Malcolm makes them earls in the last speech of the play. Five are given names, but not individual personalities. The main role of the thanes is to support whoever is in power. Ross and Lennox, for instance, are seen as supporters of Duncan in Act 1, but are present at Macbeth's feast in Act 3. When power is shifting away from Macbeth in Act 5, they are found in the armies attacking his castle. **Ross** also appears in two more intimate scenes, discussing the horrors surrounding Duncan's death with Macduff and the Old Man, and warning Lady Macduff of danger. From this we might assume that, although he is a member of Macbeth's court, he is secretly opposed to him. **Lennox** expresses similar feelings in Act 3, Scene 6.

The play also includes two English lords, Old Seyward (sometimes spelt Siward) and his son, who help to overthrow Macbeth.

Servants and the people

Most of these (attendants, doctors, murderers, soldiers, etc.) have no names, though **Seyton** emerges as an individual in Act 5. Most directors build up the role of Seyton as a distinct character, using him in the roles of attendant and messenger, sometimes even Third Murderer, earlier in the play. However, the most striking servant figure is **The Porter** who appears in only one scene (Act 2, Scene 3). The acting company to which Shakespeare belonged always contained at least one Clown and even in the tragedies we can find a 'clown part'. In *Macbeth* it consists of this one scene, a drunken, vulgar porter who is not sure if he is on Earth or in Hell. As well as amusing the audience, his lines comment on cheating, lying and deception and present Macbeth's castle as Hell. What does that make Macbeth?

Act 1, Scene 3

Plot synopsis

The Witches prepare a spell before meeting Macbeth and Banquo, victorious generals returning from battle. They speak prophecies to both men. They hail Macbeth by his title ('Thane of Glamis') and by another title which he thinks is not his ('Thane of Cawdor') before moving on to an ominous prediction.

 Third Witch All hail, Macbeth, that shalt be king hereafter!

(line 49)

Banquo is told that he will not be king, but his descendants will be. Macbeth and Banquo are puzzled by these prophecies, but news from King Duncan makes them sound more convincing. Ross and Angus inform Macbeth that the Thane of Cawdor has proved a traitor in the recent wars and that Macbeth now has the title. Macbeth is clearly tempted by the prospect of becoming King and thinks about the possibility of killing Duncan. All four thanes set off to meet King Duncan.

Text commentary

Macbeth is tempted into evil

The Witches appear very little in the play, but each of their two main appearances sets Macbeth on a course of evil. Here their predictions stir an ambition in Macbeth that brings about the murder of Duncan and Macbeth's ill-starred reign as King.

1 The prophecies

Banquo	You should be women; And yet your beards forbid me to interpret That you are so.
Macbeth	Speak if you can! What are you?
First Witch	All hail, Macbeth! Hail to thee, Thane of Glamis!
Second Witch	All hail, Macbeth! Hail to thee, Thane of Cawdor!
Third Witch	All hail, Macbeth, that shalt be king hereafter!
Banquo	Good sir, why do you start, and seem to fear Things that do sound so fair?

(lines 44–51)

Let us look at how the Weird Sisters are presented. In the early part of the scene they prepare their spell ('charm') and speak of sailing in a sieve and controlling the winds. In Banquo's descriptions of them he says that they 'look not like the inhabitants o' the earth' (line 40) and wonders if they are 'fantastical' (imaginary, line 52). See what other examples you can find of how they are presented, and consider whether Shakespeare wishes us to see them as human.

Macbeth's reaction to the Witches is very important. He is ready straight away to believe their prophecies and to think about the possibility of murder. What does he mean by his opening line (line 37)? How is the day 'foul' – in his mind, perhaps? You should remind yourself of the Witches' words in their previous scene.

 Witches Fair is foul, and foul is fair.

(1.1, line 9)

As soon as the Witches speak to him, Macbeth 'starts' (reacts sharply), and Banquo says that he is 'rapt withal' (in a trance-like state, line 56). Before the Witches vanish, Macbeth furiously pleads with them to say more. He is sorry that they have left, and he tries to find out Banquo's opinion by conversational hints. Not only before Lady Macbeth gives him courage, but even before the news of the Thane of Cawdor, Macbeth is considering his evil course of action. You should ask yourself what it is, in lines 50–51, that Macbeth fears in the apparently good news that the Witches have given him.

 In the examination you will have a copy of the scene in front of you to remind you of any quotation you need. However, it is worth learning key quotations. Examinations are against the clock and it helps to know what quotations you are looking for and where they are to be found. You may also wish to quote from another part of the play.

It seems as though the Witches are less concerned with Banquo than Macbeth. They make a prophecy to him only when he asks them.

> **Third Witch**   Thou shalt get kings, though thou be none.
>
> *(line 66)*

2 The honour

Ross
As thick as hail
Came post with post; and every one did bear
Thy praises, in his kingdom's great defence
And poured them down before him.

Angus
We are sent
To give thee from our royal master thanks;
Only to herald thee into his sight,
Not pay thee.

Ross
And, for an earnest of a greater honour,
He bade me from him call thee Thane of Cawdor
In which addition, hail, most worthy thane,
For it is thine.

(lines 96–106)

The King, by honouring Macbeth, starts the process which leads to his own death. But why should he suspect Macbeth? All the words and phrases in this section suggest two things: Duncan is firmly in power as king ('royal master', 'kingdom's great defence', etc.) and Macbeth is 'most worthy'. Macbeth, of course, has just defeated those who are disloyal; can his own loyalty be doubted?

In normal circumstances you should use formal correct English, avoiding slang and contractions (e.g. 'they've' for 'they have'). If you are writing in character, this will, of course, change, but clarity of expression is still the most important consideration.

The mood and method of expression both change totally on the entry of Ross and Angus, and again with Macbeth's **asides** weighing ambition against conscience. Ross and Angus speak in controlled and formal **blank verse**, using conventional **imagery** of courage, might and honour. The most interesting use of words is in lines 103–106. What does Ross mean by 'an earnest of a greater honour' (an 'earnest' is a pledge or promise)? Is he just exaggerating, or suggesting that the King will generally favour Macbeth from now on? We know what 'greater honour' is in the thoughts of Macbeth, the Thane of Glamis and Cawdor. When Ross says, 'hail, most worthy thane', there is even a verbal reminder of the earlier prophecies.

Macbeth's divided state of mind is well shown in his speech from lines 115 to 119. In four lines he speaks in turn to himself, to Ross and Angus and to Banquo. In each section he expresses a different view or takes a different attitude. In his first **aside** he knows what he wants: 'The greatest is behind' means that the kingship is still to come. Speaking to Ross and Angus he is polite and grateful. He then asks Banquo if he expects his children to be kings. What is he really interested in? Banquo's reply is revealing.

Banquo	That trusted home
	Might yet enkindle you unto the crown

(lines 119–120)

3 The conscience

Macbeth	This supernatural soliciting
	Cannot be ill, cannot be good. If ill,
	Why hath it given me earnest of success
	Commencing in a truth? I am Thane of Cawdor.
	If good, why do I yield to that suggestion
	Whose horrid image doth unfix my hair,
	And make my seated heart knock at my ribs
	Against the use of nature? Present fears
	Are less than horrible imaginings.

(lines 129–137)

Through all this section, Banquo and the other thanes are ready to leave, but have to wait because Macbeth is lost in thought. Banquo makes excuses for him, then finally reminds him, 'we stay upon your leisure' (line 148). What exactly is Macbeth thinking about? **Asides** express thoughts and always tell the truth.

Macbeth sees Duncan's murder as wrong and evil. 'Horrible imaginings' (thinking about the hideous deed) is only one phrase of several that tell us this: see what others you can find. Does Macbeth have any will to resist evil? Look at the word 'yield' in line 133 and, in more optimistic mood, the splendour he foresees for himself.

> Macbeth   Two truths are told
> As happy prologues to the swelling Act
> Of the imperial theme.

(lines 126–128)

Macbeth uses a metaphor from the theatre to describe the glories in store for him. The prologue preceding the main play consists of the two truths already told him: he is Thane of Glamis and Cawdor. The 'swelling Act' is the mighty theatrical experience that follows on the 'imperial theme': the subject of empire or kingship.

Timing your test essays is important. As the test proceeds, check your progress against the clock in the room. Make sure that you are giving yourself enough time to finish, but also check that you are not progressing too rapidly. If you finish very early, you have not included enough detail, so, if you realise this is going to happen, develop your arguments at greater length and add more references and quotations. Finishing 5–10 minutes early is a good idea, leaving time to check your work.

Macbeth's reaction puts his conscience at the centre of the play. He tries to weigh up good and evil, but the reason he gives for the 'supernatural soliciting' (the witches' approach to him) not being 'ill' is less than convincing: they have told two truths. Banquo understands why they have done so, even if Macbeth does not.

> Banquo   And oftentimes, to win us to our harm,
> The instruments of darkness tell us truths.

(lines 122–123)

Macbeth knows that regicide (the murder of a king) is a foul deed: just thinking about it makes his hair stand on end and his heart beat wildly. The idea is, however, well planted in his mind. The question at the end of the scene is how long his decision to do nothing (lines 142–143) will last. Even just before the murder he repeats this decision, but the temptation to his ambition is too much to resist.

Quiz

Can you fill in the background?

At the start of the play Scotland is in turmoil. Can you explain the situation and identify important characters?

a) Which country's armies invaded Scotland? What is the name of the King commanding the armies?

b) Which Scottish rebel leader led a revolt against Duncan, but has been killed by Macbeth in battle?

c) What sort of troops did the rebel lead in battle, and where were they from?

d) Which treacherous Scottish thane supported the invaders? What is his fate?

e) In the aftermath of the battle, who has to pay ten thousand dollars to Scotland? Who is made Thane of Cawdor? Who is made Prince of Cumberland?

Can you trace the plot?

Most of the major elements in the story of Macbeth (except those concerning Macduff) are first raised in this scene. Can you trace what happens later?

a) Macbeth fulfils the prophecy by killing Duncan. How does Duncan's favour help Macbeth in this deed?

b) The Witches' prophecy about Banquo also leads Macbeth into evil. How?

c) How does Macbeth express his intentions in a letter to his wife following this scene?

d) Macbeth feels a mixture of ambition and fear at the thought of killing Duncan to become king. How is his fear overcome?

e) In terms of influencing Macbeth, how are these prophecies (i) the same as, and (ii) different from, those made in Act 4, Scene 1?

Do you know these words?

Do you know the meaning of these words, all used in Act 1, Scene 3?

a) 'prosperous' (line 72)

b) 'corporal' (line 80)

c) 'vantage' (line 112)

d) 'wrought' (line 149)

e) 'fantastical' (line 52 and line 138)

f) 'ronyon' (line 6)

g) 'soliciting' (line 129)

h) 'penthouse' (line 20)

i) 'interim' (line 154)

j) 'surmise' (line 140)

Sample question

We know that Macbeth writes home to his wife soon after his meeting with the Witches. Imagine that Banquo also writes home, to his son, Fleance, explaining to him what has happened and describing his hopes, his fears and what he thinks about Macbeth's reaction. You should include:

- *your impressions of the Witches;*
- *what you think of their predictions;*
- *your opinion of Macbeth and how it changes.*

From time to time, you may be presented with a question that asks for a more creative response, like this one. Try to avoid just going through what happens in the scene. Although Banquo might want to pass on a lot of news in his letter, the examiner wants to see that you have understood the play, that you have some sense of how it works as a drama and that you have thought about the characters.

As Banquo, your impressions of the Witches may be slightly different from those of the audience, who have already seen them casting spells and talking about revenge. Nevertheless, as soon as you see the Witches you know what they are. Remember that most people at that time would believe in Witches and although you, as Banquo, may be surprised and horrified to see them, you would not necessarily react with disbelief. Banquo does say a little about what they look like, so you could expand on this, but most importantly, you need to comment on what each of them says to Macbeth and what it means. While Macbeth is so surprised that he cannot speak to them, you recover quickly and are ready to question them. Why do you react differently? 'Speak I charge you' (line 77).

The predictions the Witches make are very different for you and Macbeth. Macbeth's are very specific, very definite. He *will* become king. One of yours might seem quite clear too – 'Thou shalt get kings' – but others are much more puzzling – 'Not so happy, yet much happier' (line 66). What do you make of this? Have you any idea what they mean? Are you jealous of Macbeth, or do you treat the whole thing as a joke? Do you trust them? Does Macbeth? Although you do not know the answers to all of these questions for certain, you can make judgements based on what Macbeth says or even the look on his face, providing it fits in with everything else we know about his character.

At the beginning of this scene, Macbeth is your best friend. You have just fought a great battle together. You trust him. At the end of the scene, perhaps you are not quite so sure. Macbeth treats the predictions seriously. He has odd periods of silence, as though he is thinking things over. He does not share his thoughts with you, even though he says 'let us speak/Our free hearts each to other' (lines 154–155). Instead of being pleased at having won new honours from the king, he seems stunned. Macbeth already seems to have changed.

Remember that you can still use quotes in this kind of creative task, in reporting what Macbeth said, for example. Although his asides are supposed to be private, perhaps you overhear part of them, if you want to use them. Remember, your thoughts and feelings about Macbeth are what counts in this piece.

Act 1, Scenes 5–7

Plot synopsis

Lady Macbeth receives a letter from her husband, giving her news of the meeting with the Witches. Clearly Macbeth is thinking of becoming King, but she believes that he is not capable of wicked and decisive action and steels herself to persuade him to violence.

> *Lady Macbeth* Hie thee hither
> That I may pour my spirits in thine ear.
>
> *(1.5, lines 23–24)*

News comes that Duncan is to visit the castle, then Macbeth himself arrives, saying very little in reply to Lady Macbeth's encouragement. The arrival (Scene 6) of Duncan and the court is very pleasant, notably in the flattering and courteous words of Lady Macbeth. In Scene 7 Macbeth debates the issues and comes to the conclusion that he will take no action.

Lady Macbeth changes his mind by sheer force of her will, but also by her powers of organisation. Everything is prepared for him and he is ready to kill Duncan.

Text commentary

Macbeth commits himself to murder

The original idea to kill Duncan is Macbeth's, but there is doubt about his will to act until Lady Macbeth drives him to it. It is in these scenes that Macbeth becomes committed to a course of evil. In Scene 6 (a pleasant, if **ironic**, interlude between intense scenes) Duncan and the rest still see him as a trusted and loyal thane. However, once he has committed the first murder, further evil follows automatically.

1 Lady Macbeth soliloquises

Lady Macbeth   The raven himself is hoarse
That croaks the fatal entrance of Duncan
Under my battlements. Come, you spirits
That tend on mortal thoughts, unsex me here
And fill me from the crown to the toe top-full
Of direst cruelty. Make thick my blood;
Stop up the access and passage to remorse,
That no compunctious visitings of nature

Shake my fell purpose, nor keep peace between
The effect and it. Come to my woman's breasts
And take my milk for gall, you murdering ministers,
Wherever, in your sightless substances,
You wait on nature's mischief.

(1.5, lines 36–48)

These scenes are full of **soliloquies**, the usual way for a Shakespearean character to reveal what he or she is thinking. In Act 1, Scene 5 well over 40 of the first 52 lines feature Lady Macbeth alone, and Act 1, Scene 7 begins with a 28-line soliloquy from Macbeth. You should be able to work out why it is important to let the audience know exactly what the characters' states of mind are at this stage.

Lady Macbeth's soliloquies are terrifying in their abandonment of all natural pity or moral sense. This is the second; the first begins with her reading of the letter and her determination that Macbeth shall be king.

   Lady Macbeth   Glamis thou art, and Cawdor, and shalt be
                                   What thou art promised.

(1.5, lines 13–14)

Look at the qualities that she claims are Macbeth's failings: he is 'full o'the milk of human-kindness', he is without evil ('illness'), he wants to act 'holily' and not 'play false'. You might ask yourself whether these can really be seen as faults and also consider how often we see Macbeth act in this way during the play. Lady Macbeth knows that, in spite of these qualities, Macbeth wants to 'wrongly win', so she is confident in her powers of persuasion.

Before an examination, make sure that you revise the whole text. You will be concentrating on one scene, but will also need to make reference to other parts of the play.

The second soliloquy is even more violent than the first. News has now come of the imminent arrival of Duncan and an unexpected opportunity for instant action. Lady Macbeth begins with a telling **image** of the croaking raven, traditionally the bird of death. Then she calls on invisible devils, 'murdering ministers', to give her unnatural power. The 'spirits/That tend on mortal thoughts' are devils who wait for sinful humans to call on them. Lady Macbeth's first unnatural request is to lose her feminine qualities: soon she will be taunting Macbeth with his lack of manhood. She goes on to ask to be filled with cruelty, to feel 'no compunctious visitings of nature' (conscience) and to destroy the life-giving properties of motherhood ('gall' is bitter poison).

At the end of the play Lady Macbeth is referred to as 'fiend-like'. Here she justifies that description. Do her calling on spirits and her total acceptance of evil remind you of the Witches?

2 Macbeth soliloquises

> *Macbeth*   If it were done when 'tis done, then 'twere well
> It were done quickly. If the assassination
> Could trammel up the consequence, and catch
> With his surcease success – that but this blow
> Might be the be-all and the end-all! – here,
> But here, upon this bank and shoal of time,
> We'd jump the life to come. But in these cases
> We still have judgement here – that we but teach
> Bloody instructions, which, being taught, return
> To plague the inventor.
>
> *(1.7, lines 1–10)*

Act 1, Scene 6 offers a pleasant change from the intensity of the surrounding scenes. Macbeth is missing in that scene and, when he appears in Act 1, Scene 7 his mental agony is obvious.

This famous **soliloquy** leads to the statement, 'We will proceed no further in this business' (1.7, line 31). What are Macbeth's grounds for this decision? He raises some moral points later: as Duncan's kinsman, subject and host he should protect him, Duncan has been a virtuous and fair-minded king, and so on. However, Macbeth's first thoughts are more selfish.

The striking opening sentence, its compressed phrases bursting with energy, means, 'If the matter was finished once the deed was done, I would be happy to do it at once.' The next sentence puts the same idea in more complicated words: if the killing could prevent any consequences, Macbeth would not be worried. But what consequences is Macbeth worried about? It is not heavenly punishment troubling his conscience: Macbeth is ready to 'jump (risk) the life to come'. What worries Macbeth is that killings like this often set an example and the next victim might be the 'inventor' (himself).

> **Macbeth**   This even-handed justice
> Commends the ingredience of our poisoned chalice
> To our own lips.
>
> *(1.7, lines 10–12)*

Macbeth respects Duncan and is plagued by conscience, but his main concern is what might happen to himself afterwards.

3 Lady Macbeth inspires Macbeth's courage

> **Lady Macbeth**   I have given suck, and know
> How tender 'tis to love the babe that milks me;
> I would while it was smiling in my face
> Have plucked my nipple from his boneless gums
> And dashed the brains out, had I so sworn as you
> Have done to this.
>
> **Macbeth**   If we should fail?
>
> **Lady Macbeth**   We fail!
> But screw your courage to the sticking-place,
> And we'll not fail. When Duncan is asleep –
> Whereto the rather shall his day's hard journey
> Soundly invite him – his two chamberlains
> Will I with wine and wassail so convince
> That memory, the warder of the brain,
> Shall be a-fume, and the receipt of reason
> A limbeck only.
>
> *(1.7, lines 54–67)*

Lady Macbeth dominates the conversation with her husband. After his statement that he has decided against the murder, he attempts to defend his manhood and then, fatally, suggests the possibility of failure. This enables Lady Macbeth to argue simply that they will succeed. Soon Macbeth is unable to resist the furious confidence of her words and her deliberate loss of femininity.

> *Macbeth* Bring forth men-children only!
> For thy undaunted mettle should compose
> Nothing but males.
>
> *(1.7, lines 72–74)*

All of Lady Macbeth's speeches in this scene are dramatic and effective; the extract above (lines 54–67) is typical of her methods. The image of the baby is horrifying in itself: its life-destroying **imagery** shocks the reader or audience. It also affirms that Macbeth has made a solemn pledge to kill Duncan: when did he do this? Does Lady Macbeth's denial of her own womanhood remind you of any earlier speeches of hers?

Faced with the wavering Macbeth, Lady Macbeth next attacks him with total confidence in their success: 'We'll not fail', because she cannot even think of failure – all he needs is courage. The 'sticking place' is the notch in a cross-bow where the string is screwed tight. The **metaphor** suggests that Macbeth must wind up his courage to the maximum. Finally, Lady Macbeth is practical as well as desperately determined. She will prepare everything for Macbeth. What two purposes will be served by getting the chamberlains drunk (in the event, she drugs them as well)?

You will have long enough in your tests to prepare the essay properly. Use the reading time sensibly by deciding what are the main points you need for your essay, making a list of them and planning in what order you are going to deal with them.

The excitement and intensity of Lady Macbeth in this scene is brought out constantly in the words and **images** she uses. The description of the drunken chamberlains is a good example. The **alliteration** of 'wine' and 'wassail', the chemical **metaphor** of the fumes and the 'limbeck', and the choice of words like 'swinish', 'drenched' and 'spongy' all give a vivid impression of heightened reality. See what striking words, phrases and comparisons you can find in Lady Macbeth's attack on Macbeth's unmanly cowardice between lines 35 and 59 of Scene 7.

Quiz

Can you trace the characters?

In Act 1, Scene 6, the King's party consists of Duncan himself, seven lords (including his sons) and attendants. All are affected by the events that are about to unfold. Can you trace the part they play later in the play?

a) What similar decisions do Malcolm and Donalbain make in Act 2? How does Macbeth take advantage of these decisions?

b) What steps does Malcolm take to become King?

c) Why does Macbeth see Banquo as a threat? What action does he take as a result?

d) Do we learn anything of the parts played by Ross, Angus and Lennox in the future events?

e) What do we learn of Macduff's opinion of King Macbeth in Act 2, Scene 4?

f) How does Macbeth punish Macduff's opposition?

g) What part does Macduff play in establishing Malcolm as King?

Can you tell what happens next?

In these scenes there are many statements, especially from Lady Macbeth, about what is going to happen. Comment on whether these statements come true.

a) Before Macbeth arrives, Lady Macbeth is convinced that he will prove difficult because he is 'too full o'the milk of human-kindness' (1.5, line 15). How far is that true of his conduct in (i) Act 2, (ii) Act 3 and (iii) Act 4?

b) Lady Macbeth asks the spirits to 'unsex' her (1.5, line 39). How far does her later behaviour show this unfeminine ruthlessness she demanded?

c) 'He that's coming/Must be provided for' (1.5, lines 64–65) has two meanings. What are they and what does Lady Macbeth do to carry out both tasks?

d) Lady Macbeth says that she will make the chamberlains (guards) drunk with 'wine and wassail' (1.7, line 64) so that they cannot help Duncan. Is this what happens?

Do you know these words?

Do you know the meaning of these words, all used in Act 1, Scenes 5–7?

a) 'limbeck' (1.7, line 67)

b) 'adage' (1.7, line 45)

c) 'pendent' (1.6, line 8)

d) 'metaphysical' (1.5, line 27)

e) 'beguile' (1.5, line 61)

f) 'procreant' (1.6, line 8)

g) 'surcease' (1.7, line 4)

h) 'wassail' (1.7, line 64)

i) 'dunnest' (1.5, line 49)

j) 'coign' (1.6, line 7)

Sample question

In these scenes, we are shown that people have very different opinions of Macbeth. Describe and explain what people think of him. You will need to look at:

- *the way Lady Macbeth talks about him before he arrives and what she says to him;*

- *King Duncan's approach to him;*

- *the way Macbeth feels about himself;*

- *the way the audience feels about him.*

In your introduction, talk about the way Shakespeare deliberately puts these scenes next to each other to create a contrast of moods. We get ideas about darkness and evil next to images of light and happiness, confusion and uncertainty next to confidence and careful planning.

For much of Scene 5, Lady Macbeth is alone and we can therefore be sure that what she says is really what she thinks and feels. Have a look at her speech from about line 14. What exactly does she mean when she says 'Yet do I fear thy nature: It is too full o' th' milk of human kindness'? It does not just mean she thinks Macbeth is too soft. Pick out some of the other words she uses to describe Macbeth, such as 'highly', 'holily' and 'great Glamis'. What do these suggest she thinks? Why does she want to 'pour my spirits in thine ear'?

As soon as Duncan arrives he creates a warm, friendly atmosphere by the way he describes the castle. He continues to make us think he has a high opinion of both Macbeth and his wife, describing her as 'Fair and noble' and saying 'we love him highly'. You can point out that Duncan does not know all the things we know about Macbeth. He has only seen loyalty and bravery.

In Scene 7, Macbeth shares his own thoughts with us. He wants to become king, but he knows killing Duncan is wrong. He gives several reasons for thinking this. What are they? When he talks about 'Vaulting ambition', what does it tell us?

The audience knows a lot that the characters do not. We know exactly how Macbeth feels about killing Duncan. We know how confused he feels about the murder he has planned. We know just how soon after meeting the Witches the idea first occurred to him. We also know things that only some of the characters know, such as just how much pressure his wife has put him under, or the sense of pride and honour he felt at the end of the battle. We can use all of these different views to make a more balanced judgement about him. His wife does not understand why he hesitates, what it is that stops him from killing Duncan. Explain these reasons. You can mention here how some of the other characters feel about Macbeth. Banquo, for example is his closest friend and was with him when he met the Witches.

Finish the essay by giving your own opinion of Macbeth. What do you like and dislike about him?

Act 2, Scenes 2–3

Plot synopsis

Macbeth commits the murder of Duncan off-stage as Lady Macbeth waits. Eventually Macbeth returns, shaken with guilt. Lady Macbeth has two problems with him, a practical one and an emotional one. She must return the daggers he has brought with him and smear the guards with blood. She must also persuade him to conceal his guilt and make a good impression in front of the court.

> *Lady Macbeth* A little water clears us of this deed.
>
> *(2.2, line 67)*

Macduff is heard knocking at the castle gate: he has come to wait on Duncan. After the brief comic scene with the Porter, Macduff enters with Lennox. The discovery of Duncan's dead body leads to a rapid sequence of events. The alarm bells sound, all the court assembles, and Macbeth goes to view the body and kills the guards, claiming to be furious at the murder they have committed. Lady Macbeth faints at a time of difficult questioning for Macbeth. As all the other lords prepare to assemble in the hall, Duncan's sons decide to flee.

Text commentary

Macbeth seizes power

Although Macbeth is not confirmed as King in these scenes, he has done what is necessary to gain the Crown, and in the next scene it is stated that he has been named King. Oddly there seems to be little real opposition: Macduff confines his distrust to words and Malcolm and Donalbain offer no challenge. However, Macbeth seems anything but a bold and hardened murderer.

1 Macbeth's conscience plagues him

Macbeth	Still it cried 'Sleep no more' to all the house: 'Glamis hath murdered sleep, and therefore Cawdor Shall sleep no more – Macbeth shall sleep no more.'
Lady Macbeth	Who was it that thus cried? Why worthy thane, You do unbend your noble strength to think So brain-sickly of things – go get some water, And wash this filthy witness from your hand. Why did you bring these daggers from the place? They must lie there – go carry them, and smear The sleepy grooms with blood.

(2.2, lines 41–50)

The build-up of terror in these scenes is acute. Sound effects and off-stage noises increase the tension. In the previous scene Macbeth waits for the bell to signal that all is ready, then it sounds and he exits. Macbeth and Lady Macbeth constantly think they are hearing noises in Scene 2, and Lady Macbeth's **soliloquy** (lines 1–8) refers to the 'fatal' sound of the owl. At the end of Scene 2, moving into Scene 3, the knocking serves as a threat of discovery. However, the unhinged state of Macbeth's mind is the main reason for tension. Just before the murder he has spoken perhaps his most famous soliloquy, which shows him hallucinating in his guilt.

Macbeth Is this a dagger which I see before me,
The handle toward my hand?

(2.1, lines 33–34)

Most of Scene 2 is taken up with the urgent promptings of Lady Macbeth to her husband so that he will not betray the crime by acts of folly (like taking away the daggers) or a public breakdown. His guilt is expressed mainly through the twin **images** of sleep and blood. The two are seen as opposites, representing peace/innocence and violence/guilt. He imagines hearing a voice that tells him that he will never sleep again: in other words, he will never be free of the guilt of his deeds. Notice the way that lines 42–43 use his titles in turn. What does this remind you of?

Macbeth sees himself as outside Christian forgiveness: he cannot say 'Amen' and ask for God's blessing. All Lady Macbeth can say in reply is to tell him not to think about it. Read the quotation below and consider its importance to the later development of the characters of the Macbeths.

Lady Macbeth These deeds must not be thought
After these ways; so, it will make us mad.

(2.2, lines 33–34)

Lady Macbeth takes a different response to the 'blood' **image**. After all, Macbeth is standing there with blood on his hands and must

33

cleanse himself before anyone sees him. So she is much more practical: she tells him to wash his hands and tries to force him to smear the grooms with blood. It is possible to wash off actual blood. Is it possible to wash off the guilt of the blood? Lady Macbeth claims so, and even mocks Macbeth for his 'white' (pale, cowardly) heart in contrast to his red hands.

> Macbeth   No, this my hand will rather
> The multitudinous seas incarnadine.
>
> *(2.2, lines 61–62)*

To Macbeth there is no power sufficient to remove the blood/guilt. Notice the way that Shakespeare uses enormously long words as though to suggest that he is writing of mighty things: the blood on his hands is so powerful that it can turn the world's oceans red.

It is essential that you read the question very carefully and make sure that you answer all parts of it. Probably there will be a list of suggestions of what you might include in the essay. You do not have to plan your essay around these points, but they are very helpful in pointing you towards useful material.

The pacing of these scenes is crucial. Though desperately urgent, the opening of Scene 2 is slowed by Lady Macbeth's soliloquy and the bewildered entrance of Macbeth. As the scene ends, the knocking increases the tempo and Lady Macbeth is increasingly concerned that they act quickly to conceal their actions, retiring to their bedroom in case they are revealed as 'watchers' (still awake and active). As the knocking becomes more frequent, the audience identifies with the Macbeths' race against time. Then, suddenly, the Porter enters and the pace slows.

2 Comic relief and unnatural omens

> Porter   Knock, knock! Who's there in the other devil's name?
> Faith, here's an equivocator that could swear in both
> the scales against each scale, who committed treason

enough for God's sake, yet could not equivocate to heaven. O, come in, equivocator.

(2.3, lines 7–11)

You might wonder why Shakespeare included the porter scene which consists of a fairly short **soliloquy** to the accompaniment of knocking at the gate, followed by an equally short dialogue with Macduff full of coarse jokes about drunkenness. The explanations are many. In practical terms, Shakespeare's company employed at least one clown at any time and all the great tragedies contain a part for him, even if it is as short as the Porter's. Here he serves the purpose of providing relief between the varied horrors of the murder and the discovery, and also allows enough time to pass for the Macbeths to go to their chamber, clean up and, possibly, change clothes.

The crimes the Porter deals with do not particularly relate to Macbeth, although the 'equivocator' who commits treason has some resemblance to him. An equivocator is a liar who swears things to be true which he does not believe. You might like to consider the following questions: What effect does it have at this time to list criminals condemned to Hell? What is achieved by making Macbeth's Porter imagine himself the Porter at Hell-gate?

 Lennox   The obscure bird
Clamoured the live-long night. Some say the earth
Was feverous and did shake.

(2.3, lines 57–58)

In *Macbeth* the evil deeds of mankind are linked to a wider world of evil, notably through the Witches. Here, Lennox's speech in lines 51–58 (made before the discovery of the dead Duncan) presents a world which is sick and out of order. Note that the earth itself shakes with fever.' 'Twas a rough night' indeed, as Macbeth remarks with much understatement, but, more than that, the events are uncanny, predicting a time of woe. Note particularly the adjectives 'strange', 'terrible', 'dire' and 'confused', all within three lines.

part of a pattern. 'The obscure bird' is the owl, thought to ᵉath: find two references to the sound of the owl in the ᵉne and think how they contribute to the atmosphere. As orms and unnatural events, Scene 4 is full of them, ᵃⁿ owl (again) killing a falcon (lines 11–13). The impression is that the prospect of Macbeth's murder of Duncan, and the murder itself, have disturbed the whole fabric of human life and nature. You will notice that Macduff refers to death as 'The Great Doom's image' (2.3, line 75); it is as though the Day of Judgement has arrived.

In reading the question take note of key words which instruct you in what to do. If you are asked to compare, you must find similarities and differences between two or more things. If asked to explain, you must show why. Do not automatically tell the story, though you may need to include some narration if you are asked to 'give an account'.

The impression given by this scene is, thus, that what has happened is more than a murder, even more than regicide (killing a king). The Porter is at Hell-gate, the earth is sick of a fever, men are turned to stone, the Last Judgement is here – a universal force of evil and death has been let loose.

3 Macbeth escapes accusation

Macbeth   Here lay Duncan,
His silver skin laced with his golden blood,
And his gashed stabs looked like a breach in nature
For ruin's wasteful entrance; there the murderers,
Steeped in the colours of their trade, their daggers
Unmannerly breeched with gore. Who could refrain,
That had a heart to love, and in that heart
Courage to make's love known?

(2.3, lines 108–115)

Macbeth receives unwelcome attention when Macduff questions him about why he killed the supposed murderers. Macbeth's defence is based upon his loyalty to, and love for, Duncan. Lady Macbeth's advice to him on keeping up appearances has been heeded. Previously (lines 88–93) he has suggested that there is nothing left for him now that Duncan is dead. Now he apologises (lines 103–104), but defends himself as being too impetuous in his love for Duncan. Once again, the emphasis on blood dominates the speech: apart from the word 'blood' itself, you should be able to find at least three other clear references.

It is surprising, however, that Macbeth's explanation is so readily accepted, even with the assistance of Lady Macbeth's diversion when her fainting is followed by Macduff and Banquo, gentlemen both, being distracted in identical words, 'Look to the lady!'.

Lady Macbeth (swooning)   Help me hence, ho!

(2.3, line 115)

There are reasons to suspect that both Macduff and the King's sons have their doubts about Macbeth, but none of them takes a positive role in uncovering the murderer. Malcolm responds assertively to the news of his father's murder ('O, by whom?', line 97), but neither he nor his brother speaks another line in public.

Malcolm (to Donalbain) Why do we hold our tongues,
                           That most may claim this argument
                           for ours?

(2.3, lines 116–117)

As Donalbain's reply shows, they are afraid that their 'fate' may rush upon them: they, too, may be murdered. Oddly, the thanes seem to ignore them, even Macduff who becomes Malcolm's closest ally later. As for Macduff, he joins Banquo in swearing to fight treason, but in the next scene he is already cutting himself off from court politics. Macbeth escapes investigation, but these scenes also make clear that he cannot escape imprisonment in his own guilt and evil.

Quiz

Can you trace the character?

Macbeth's character undergoes great changes during the play, especially at this point when the murder of Duncan is successful. Can you find suitable quotations to mark these changes?

a) When he is accosted by the Witches, he is tempted, but fears the evil involved. Can you find two quotations from Act 1, Scene 3 to prove this?

b) What does Lady Macbeth think will be Macbeth's weakness? Find a quotation from Act 1, Scene 5.

c) Find a quotation that expresses Macbeth's horror at the planned murder (2.1).

d) Find a quotation in Act 2, Scene 2 that expresses Macbeth's regret at what he has done.

e) By Act 3, Scene 2 Macbeth no longer needs his wife's encouragement. What words prove this?

f) Macbeth is trapped in his own evil. What quotation from Act 3, Scene 4 suggests that he is committing murders simply because he is unable to escape from his own villainy?

g) By the end the whole matter of fame and glory, even life itself, counts for little. Which speech in Act 5, Scene 5 sums up the pointlessness of all he has done?

Can you explain the image?

a) In Act 2, Scene 2, lines 55–57, Lady Macbeth says that, if Duncan bleeds, she will 'gild the faces of the grooms' to suggest their 'guilt'. Can you explain the **pun** in these lines?

b) Donalbain says (2.3, lines 137–138), 'The nea'er (nearer) in blood/The nearer bloody.' Can you explain the two meanings of 'blood' as he uses them?

c) What do you think is the significance of the 'anointed temple' **metaphor** in Act 2, Scene 3, lines 62–65?

d) Macbeth uses many **metaphors** about 'sleep'. Can you explain what 'great nature's second course' (2.2, line 39) means?

Do you know these words?

Do you know the meaning of these words, all used in Act 2, Scenes 2–3?

a) 'surfeited' (2.2, line 5)

b) 'multitudinous' (2.2, line 62)

c) 'auger-hole' (2.3, line 119)

d) 'Gorgon' (2.3, line 69)

e) 'combustion' (2.3, line 55)

f) 'sleave' (2.2, line 37)

g) 'undivulged' (2.3, line 128)

h) 'physics' (2.3, line 47)

i) 'possets' (2.2, line 6)

j) 'parley' (2.3, line 79)

Sample question

How does Shakespeare make the events in these two scenes seem very dramatic? You should comment on:

- *how the language is used to create mood;*
- *the importance of what we see and what we do not see;*
- *the contrasts between different characters.*

In your introduction, you could talk about the importance of killing the king. How does Macbeth show that he knows it is wrong? Why would an audience in Shakespeare's time be particularly horrified? The play has been building up to this moment since almost the first line. The audience knows it is going to happen but is willing Macbeth to see sense and stop.

When the scene opens, Lady Macbeth is alone on stage, which means we share her fears and anxieties. She tries to give the impression that she is full of confidence, but she cannot help being startled by the smallest sound. The fact that we can imagine what is happening in Duncan's room, but we cannot see it, makes it very tense. Then Macbeth appears, his hands covered in blood, clutching the daggers. Our attention is focused on the blood, not the body, which we never see. This makes it seem all the more horrible. After this, every time Macbeth – or anyone else – mentions blood, this is what we think of. You could include here a quote about blood from elsewhere in the play.

Later, in Scene 3, when Macduff arrives, the audience's attention stays on Macbeth, pretending to be calm and acting normally, while Macduff goes to discover the body. The audience knows what Macbeth is really thinking and feeling.

There are a lot of clear differences between the characters. Macbeth is deeply shocked by what he has done, but he was still able to commit the murder. Lady Macbeth could not kill Duncan, and at first seems very frightened, but then takes charge and seems more in control of herself: 'Infirm of purpose! Give me the daggers' (2.2, lines 52–53). Later, it becomes more complicated. When Macduff arrives, he is grief stricken, but Macbeth only pretends to feel the same. We can see the difference. You also need to look at the different ways that Macbeth and Lady Macbeth deal with the voice Macbeth says he heard saying 'Sleep no more' (2.2, line 35). There is a contrast too, between the vulgar jokes of the Porter and the terrible events that have taken place.

Since we do not see Duncan's body, Shakespeare uses language in various ways to suggest to the audience some of the horror of the scenes. Look at some of the places he breaks sentences up into short sharp sections, or uses exclamations 'Th'attempt and not the deed/Confounds us. – Hark!' (2.2, lines 10–11)

Find some of the references to animals doing unnatural things and explain why they are included. Look at the different ways the word 'blood' is used. Pick out some of the references to anger, fear, nervousness and horror. All of these feelings help make the scene more dramatic.

In your conclusion, explain briefly how the dramatic events in these scenes lead to Macbeth's destruction.

Act 3, Scene 4

Plot synopsis

The banquet that the King and Queen are holding for the court is about to begin when the First Murderer reports to Macbeth. Banquo, he says, is dead, but his son, Fleance, has escaped. Macbeth thus suffers from guilt with only a slight reduction in his fears. He attempts to conceal his feelings by blaming Banquo for his absence and talking of his great friendship with him. When he mentions the name, Banquo's Ghost appears and Macbeth's guilt surfaces.

> **Macbeth** Thou canst not say I did it; never shake
> Thy gory locks at me.

(lines 49–50)

Macbeth's sanity seems in doubt and the situation is only saved by Lady Macbeth. She attempts to restrain his outbursts without much success, but manages to think of excuses and dismisses the thanes speedily. Macbeth, emotionally shattered and becoming weary of sin, resolves to go to see the Witches.

Text commentary

Macbeth loses control

Macbeth has not always been in control of himself before, but, with the aid of Lady Macbeth, he has kept up appearances. Now his behaviour shows him to be either guilty or crazy or both. This is the last time that the court meets in a civilised manner. Macbeth trusts in the Witches and the next time the action returns to his castle in Act 5 only servants (including a doctor) seem to remain.

1 The Queen in charge

> **Lady Macbeth** O proper stuff!
> This is the very painting of your fear.
> This is the air-drawn dagger which you said
> Led you to Duncan. O, these flaws and starts,
> Impostors to true fear, would well become
> A woman's story at a winter's fire,
> Authorized by her grandam. Shame itself!
> Why do you make such faces? When all's done
> You look but on a stool.

(lines 59–67)

Shakespeare's presentation of Lady Macbeth is interesting and unusual. At the time of Duncan's murder she is dominant and heartless, almost living up to Malcolm's description of her at the end of the play as 'fiend-like'. By the start of Act 3 she has been marginalised: that is, Macbeth no longer includes her in his plans. Her only appearance later in the play is in a state of helpless madness. This is the last we see of the determined woman we saw in Acts 1 and 2, and you should compare her words and actions then and now.

This speech reminds us of Act 2, Scene 1 ('Is this a dagger...'). Her reaction here recalls her treatment of Macbeth before Duncan's murder. Her reference to the old wives' tale casts doubt on Macbeth's masculinity. See what examples you can find between Act 1, Scene 5 and Act 2, Scene 2 where Lady Macbeth insults his manhood or denies her own femininity.

At the end of a test essay it is useful to sum up your opinions with a conclusion. However, it is more important to keep your main argument in view throughout, and simply repeating yourself in a lengthy concluding paragraph gains little credit.

You will find that Lady Macbeth's language is similar to that she uses in earlier scenes. We are reminded of ' 'Tis the eye of childhood/ That fears a painted devil' (2.2, lines 54–55). Lady Macbeth's conduct in this scene follows her own instructions in Act 1, Scene 5 to 'bear welcome in the eye' and 'look like the innocent flower'. From the moment of the First Murderer's departure she is using her charm to keep up appearances with the lords.

 Lady Macbeth Sit, worthy friends. My lord is often thus.

(line 52)

She constantly uses words like 'friends', 'cheer', 'mirth' and 'pleasure' to show what a cheerful gathering this is – or should be. You can find many examples of Macbeth acting similarly, pretending to be humble, at the start of the scene, but his attempts do not last long, unlike the Queen's.

At the very end of the scene she excuses Macbeth using one of the key **images** of the play: he lacks sleep. The loss of sleep or of its benefits, because of guilt, is constantly emphasised. Look, for instance, at Macbeth's words in Act 2, Scene 2, lines 35–43 and at the next appearance of Lady Macbeth (5.1) when her power and self-control have disappeared.

2 The Ghost: 'blood-boltered Banquo'

Enter Ghost

Macbeth   I drink to the general joy o'the whole table,
And to our dear friend Banquo, whom we miss.
Would he were here! To all – and him – we thirst,
And all to all.

Lords   Our duties and the pledge!

Macbeth (sees the Ghost) Avaunt, and quit my sight! Let
the earth hide thee!
Thy bones are marrowless, thy blood is cold.
Thou hast no speculation in those eyes
Which thou dost glare with.

(lines 88–95)

What is this ghost? Is it real or a product of Macbeth's diseased imagination? Notice that, on both its appearances, Macbeth sees it when he is talking about Banquo: the murdered man is in his mind. Notice also that it disappears when Macbeth plucks up courage to resist it. Nobody else can see it, so is it like the 'air-drawn dagger', all in Macbeth's mind? On the other hand, belief in victims returning as ghosts to torment their murderers was very strong at the time and such ghosts always appeared only to the guilty ones.

The appearance of the Ghost prompts Macbeth's terror and guilt. Throughout the play guilt is expressed by **imagery** of blood. You will recall striking examples from such scenes as the first murder and Lady Macbeth's sleep-walking.

Macbeth   Will all great Neptune's ocean wash this blood
          Clean from my hand?

(2.2, lines 60-61)

Lady Macbeth Here's the smell of the blood still.

(5.1, line 48)

Blood is connected with every mention of the dead Banquo and with Macbeth's feelings of guilt. Banquo's blood is on the Murderer's face; the ghost's hair is 'gory' (bloody); in Act 4, Scene 1 the apparition of Banquo is 'blood-boltered'. There are many more references to blood for you to find in Act 3, Scene 4. Perhaps the most important, but by no means the only ones, express Macbeth's guilt late in the scene. He is 'the secret'st man of blood' (line 125) whose guilt will be revealed. He has waded so far in blood that he despairs of being able to return (lines 135–137). Macbeth is committed to blood, murders and guilt; he knows it will lead to suffering, but he cannot stop.

Macbeth   It will have blood, they say; blood will have blood.

(line 121)

3 Macbeth: man of courage?

Macbeth   What man dare, I dare.
            Approach thou like the rugged Russian bear,
            The armed rhinoceros, or the Hyrcan tiger,
            Take any shape but that, and my firm nerves
            Shall never tremble. Or be alive again,
            And dare me to the desert with thy sword:
            If trembling I inhabit then, protest me
            The baby of a girl.

(lines 98–105)

Many contrasting comments are made on Macbeth's courage during the play. In battle at the beginning he is 'brave Macbeth' (repeated many times in different words), but soon Lady Macbeth is accusing him of lacking manhood. The opening line here reminds us of 'I dare do all that may become a man' (1.7, line 47), when Lady Macbeth is calling him a coward. His fears appear in this scene even before the Ghost appears: 'Then comes my fit (of fear or anxiety) again' (line 20) is his response to the escape of Fleance. Nevertheless the audience believes him when he says that he would face wild beasts without trembling (incidentally, Hyrcania on the Caspian Sea was, in Roman times, the traditional home of the tiger, hence 'the Hyrcan tiger'). In battle, even in doomed combat with Macduff, Macbeth is always courageous.

What Macbeth is afraid of is his own evil and anything prompting him to further evil. He is also afraid of threats to the security which he hoped to gain by his evil deeds. The news of Fleance tells him that a rival for the throne exists and that his latest crime may need to be repeated. Banquo's Ghost is a 'horrible shadow' that terrifies him.

 You should be able to make sure that you finish your essay in the test. However, if you run out of time before you have made all the points you want to, spend the last five minutes jotting down in note form what you intended to write. It is not ideal, but it is better than leaving them out altogether.

Macbeth's protests about all the dangers he would face seem rather hysterical, as do many of his responses in this scene. Look, for example, at his speeches about the return of the dead, even with 'twenty mortal murders on their crowns' (line 80): in other words, twenty wounds each sufficient to kill the victim.

 Macbeth   If charnel-houses and our graves must send
Those that we bury, back, our monuments
Shall be the maws of kites.

(lines 70–72)

This difficult quotation means that, if the dead persist in returning from normal burial-places, bodies will have to be fed to the birds – an **image** that shows how disturbed Macbeth's imagination is. Equally hysterical is the speech about how everything unites in revealing the guilt of the 'man of blood' (lines 121–125).

Let us examine how Macbeth has changed by the end of the scene. He is desperate and plagued by guilt, but these are not the only changes. What does the statement that he keeps 'a servant fee'd (paid)' in every lord's house show about his method of ruling?

Whom does he now turn to for advice and help, instead of his wife? Acts 1 and 2 were about his overthrow of Duncan, Act 3 about the murder of Banquo. Who is the new enemy who is now opposing him (lines 127–129)?

The most ominous change is his approach to his own feelings of guilt. He now believes that his fears and his doubts can be overcome by yet further crimes. Shakespeare even uses a rhyming **couplet** to make the point more strongly.

Macbeth   My strange and self-abuse
Is the initiate fear that wants hard use.

(lines 141–142)

Quiz

Can you trace the character?

This is the last scene in which Lady Macbeth plays an important part in influencing the conduct of her husband. Can you trace her role throughout the play?

a) Lady Macbeth receives a letter from Macbeth in Act 1, Scene 5, suggesting that he might become King. What does she think may stand in the way of his ambition?

b) She says, 'Leave all the rest to me' (1.5, line 71). What does she do to help Macbeth in the murder of Duncan? Mention three things.

c) What does she do to distract attention from Macbeth after the discovery of Duncan's body?

d) What part does she play in planning Banquo's murder?

e) In her final appearance she says, 'All the perfumes of Arabia will not sweeten this little hand' (5.1, lines 48–49). What words that she speaks in Act 2, Scene 2 does this contradict?

Can you find the image?

This scene contains many examples of images which Shakespeare uses throughout the play. Can you supply the missing word in each of the following quotations and suggest what idea it conveys?

a) 'There the grown ... lies.'

b) 'I am in .../Stepped in so far.'

c) 'You lack the season of all natures, ...'.

d) 'The ... is momentary.'

e) 'Are you a ... ?'

Do you know these words?

Do you know the meaning of these words, all used in Act 3, Scene 4?

a) 'blanched' (line 115)

b) 'maggot-pies and choughs' (line 124)

c) 'nonpareil' (line 18)

d) 'maws' (line 72)

e) 'Weird' (line 132)

f) 'initiate' (line 142)

g) 'charnel-houses' (line 70)

h) 'cabined' (line 23)

i) 'trenched' (line 26)

j) 'roofed' (lines 39)

Sample question

How does Macbeth change in this scene? You should consider:

- *what he is like at the beginning of the scene and why;*
- *what he is like at the end of the scene;*
- *his relationship with his wife;*
- *the effect Banquo's ghost has on him.*

In your introduction, you should explain that this scene is one of the most important parts of the whole play, because this is where Macbeth realises he can never go back to being the man he was before Duncan's murder.

At the beginning of the scene Macbeth is nervous, but still fairly sure of himself. How do the first speeches in the scene show how he is feeling? He knows it is important that he should impress his guests. How does he try to do so? Explain how his mood changes from optimism to despair and back again, when he goes to talk to the murderer.

At the end of the scene, look at Macbeth's final words, 'we are yet but young in deed' (line 143). Explain what he means by this. Having realised he can never forget what he has done, he decides to go on killing, to kill before he has had time to think about it. Look at the way he speaks about murder: 'I am in blood stepped in so far...', and explain how he feels about it now. He seems to have found a new determination. How does he show it? Pick out lines you can use as proof.

When looking at the relationship between Macbeth and his wife, you need to point out just how close they were earlier in the play. Now, at the beginning of this scene, Macbeth is already so concerned with his own problems that he has started to leave his wife out of his plans. How does Lady Macbeth feel at this point? Is she worried? Afraid? What evidence can you find to support your ideas? Later in the scene, Lady Macbeth tries to cover up for her husband, making excuses for his bizarre behaviour. By the end of the scene Macbeth has left her behind. She is still pretending nothing has happened, while he plans more murders: 'Blood will have blood'.

The appearance of the ghost makes Macbeth realise he can never hide what he has done from himself. The first time it appears, he shrinks away from it, 'Thou canst not say I did it' (Line 49); by the time it appears again, his attitude has changed, 'Hence horrible shadow!' (line 105). Why does he feel differently? Does the fact that only he can see it make a difference?

In your conclusion, talk about how this turning point affects the rest of the play. We only see Lady Macbeth one more time. Why? Events seem to gather more speed as Macbeth tries to keep control of his life. Macbeth relies more on what the Witches tell him. As the people around him start to distrust Macbeth, they become more determined to do something about it. Explain briefly how all this affects what happens next.

Act 4, Scene 1

Plot synopsis

Macbeth has already decided that he needs the advice of the Weird Sisters. Before he arrives, the three Witches prepare a suitably grotesque mixture in their cauldron to aid their charms. Hecate and a number of other witches appear, but the main section of the scene concerns the apparitions that arise from the cauldron. The first brings a warning.

 First Apparition   Macbeth, Macbeth, Macbeth: beware Macduff.

(line 70)

However, the other two give him confidence, suggesting that he cannot be killed or conquered, but Macbeth's relief does not last long. A parade of Scottish kings stretches out into the future, all pointed out by Banquo's Ghost as his descendants. The Witches disappear, Macbeth returns to reality and Lennox arrives with news of the flight of Macduff to England. Macbeth decides to take evil one stage further: he will slaughter the Thane of Fife's family.

Text commentary

Macbeth deceived by the Witches

In this scene the witches again appear as the enemies of Macbeth, though pretending to help him. They do as he asks, but in a way that produces in him a fatal mixture of fear and confidence and leads him to further, worse evil.

1 The Witches prepare

Second Witch	Fillet of a fenny snake
	In the cauldron boil and bake;
	Eye of newt, and toe of frog,
	Wool of bat, and tongue of dog,
	Adder's fork, and blind-worm's sting,
	Lizard's leg, and howlet's wing,
	For a charm of powerful trouble,
	Like a hell-broth, boil and bubble.
All	Double, double, toil and trouble;
	Fire burn and cauldron bubble.

(lines 12–21)

The Witches appear twice to tempt Macbeth into evil. Each scene contains a section before they meet him which convinces us of their unearthly strangeness and their evil intentions towards mankind. In this case they are seen mixing the charm which will reveal the apparitions to Macbeth. The effect is gained partly through animal **imagery**. In the opening lines they refer to their animal familiars: a cat, a hedgehog and the mysterious 'Harpier', possibly a 'harpy', a sort of mythical evil spirit in the form of a bird-woman.

Soon they are listing 'the ingredience (ingredients) of our cauldron'. See how many animals or plants you can identify which are associated with poison, evil or danger. In the Third Witch's speech (lines 22 onwards) parts of human beings join the horrifying brew. Particularly unpleasant is the finger of a baby who has been strangled after being born in a ditch to a prostitute.

When you plan your essay, make a clear decision about what each paragraph is going to be about. If at all possible, make it clear what the subject or topic of the paragraph is in the first sentence, often called a 'topic sentence'.

The strangeness of the Witches is also brought out by the difference in the verse that they use. Most of the verse in the play is **blank verse**, but the Witches speak in rhyming **couplets**. See what other difference you can find in the verse. Compare the following lines.

Second Witch Cool it with a baboon's blood,
Then the charm is firm and good.

(lines 37–38)

Macbeth I conjure you, by that which you profess.

(line 49)

Another element in the strangeness of the Witches is that they speak as one unit rather than individuals. The most famous lines in this scene, 'Double, double, toil and trouble,/Fire burn and cauldron bubble,' are spoken by all three together, probably as they move round the cauldron, and they are constantly repeated as a spell or charm. Notice how the three also echo each other: each speaks to her familiar, then each adds to the mixture, later each invites Macbeth to speak (line 60) and so on. Whatever effects are used, the audience should feel that the Witches are otherworldly and menacing, a mood continued by Macbeth's greeting, 'How now, you secret, black and midnight hags?' (line 47).

2 Macbeth and the apparitions

> *Macbeth*   Filthy hags,
> Why do you show me this? – A fourth? Start, eyes!
> What, will the line stretch out to the crack of doom?
> Another yet? A seventh? I'll see no more!
> And yet the eighth appears, who bears a glass
> Which shows me many more. And some I see
> That two-fold balls and treble sceptres carry.
> Horrible sight! Now I see 'tis true,
> For the blood-boltered Banquo smiles upon me,
> And points at them for his.
>
> *(lines 114–123)*

Macbeth has greeted two of the apparitions' prophecies with pleasure and relief ('sweet bodements good'), but now, at the end of the scene, he despairs. Let us look back at all four apparitions and see how the Witches have manipulated his feelings. The First Apparition, an armed head (a man in armour: Macduff?), tells him to beware Macduff: straightforward advice that Macbeth accepts.

The next two deceive Macbeth with words that suggest that he is safe. You should be able to work out why 'a bloody child' stands for Macduff and 'a child crowned, with a tree in his hand' represents Malcolm. Their predictions apparently say that Macbeth can never be hurt or defeated.

> *Second Apparition*   none of woman born
> Shall harm Macbeth.
>
> *(lines 79–80)*

Third Apparition Macbeth shall never vanquished be, until
Great Birnam Wood to high Dunsinane Hill
Shall come against him.

(lines 91–93)

It is important to note who the speakers are: Macduff is the man, not born of woman, who will kill Macbeth and Malcolm is the man who will move Birnam Wood against him. Of course the audience do not know this in Act 4 and it shocks us as much as Macbeth when the predictions work out in Act 5. The moment Macbeth is told of the moving wood (5.5) or hears that Macduff 'was from his mother's womb/Untimely ripped' (5.6, lines 54–55), he knows that he is doomed. The Witches' trickery has triumphed.

Quotations are useful in an examination essay, but should be kept fairly short. You should quote a line or two, set out on the page as in the text, or fit a few words into your own sentence, identifying the quotation with speech-marks.

Even before the Witches' trickery becomes obvious, they create an apparition that drives out all Macbeth's hope. Their reply to his question whether Banquo's descendants will ever reign is a parade of kings. Macbeth's commentary tells of an apparently never-ending line (thanks to the glass or mirror) presided over by Banquo. Why is Banquo described as 'blood-boltered'? What crime did Macbeth commit to keep the succession in his family? Note the reference to uniting the Crowns of Scotland (which had orb and sceptre) and England (which had one orb and two sceptres). James VI of Scotland, who became King of England in 1603 (a few years before Shakespeare wrote *Macbeth*), was doubtless very flattered by the reference.

You should note how Shakespeare suggests that Macbeth is unbalanced by all the broken sentences, questions and exclamations. The reference to 'the crack of doom' (the end of the world, Judgement Day) helps to put the scene outside the ordinary world. The language is full of words like 'horrible' and 'filthy', and 'blood' is one of the key words in the play. Investigate how many uses you can find of blood in this scene, but also reflect on its importance as an **image** of guilt in scenes like Act 2, Scene 2, Act 3, Scene 4 and Act 5, Scene 1.

3 Macbeth decides

Macbeth (aside) From this moment,

The very firstlings of my heart shall be
The firstlings of my brain. And even now,
To crown my thoughts with acts, be it thought and done:
The castle of Macduff I will surprise,
Seize upon Fife, give to the edge o' the sword
His wife, his babes, and all unfortunate souls
That trace him in his line. No boasting like a fool;
This deed I'll do, before this purpose cool.
But no more sights!

(lines 145–154)

An **aside**, like a **soliloquy**, can be taken as expressing the truthful thoughts of the speaker. Macbeth has had enough of 'sights': he may be confident enough in Act 5, Scene 6 to jeer at opponents who cannot kill him, but the apparitions have terrified him and made his power meaningless. He is also changed in his attitude to killing. Think back to the murder of Duncan and then that of Banquo and compare them both to his decision to kill off Macduff's wife and 'babes'. How has Macbeth changed in the course of play, and why?

Examiners know that you are writing against the clock and understand that there will be some errors of spelling, punctuation, etc. However, if you have time, it is always worthwhile to check your completed work thoroughly to reduce mistakes to a minimum.

It is interesting to consider where this scene may take place. The Witches are present before Macbeth and he has decided to visit them, so are they on the heath again? Macbeth, though, calls to Lennox (line 134), 'Come in, without (outside) there' which suggests it is an inside scene, as does the Second Witch's 'Open locks, whoever knocks' (line 46). The Witches are perfectly at home, then they vanish and we are in the real world in which messengers gallop up on horses. All this increases the otherworldly impression of the Witches. Particularly important is the use of words like 'pernicious' and 'curse' which link them to hell and damnation.

> **Macbeth** Infected be the air whereon they ride,
> And damned all those who trust them.

(lines 137–138)

Is the second line of this quotation literally true? To whom would you apply it?

Let us think about the consequences of Macbeth's visit to the Witches. The murder of the Macduff family is the result of the prophecies and the news of Macduff's departure for England. It provides a turning-point in many ways: think of the effect on Macbeth himself, on Macduff and, possibly indirectly, on Lady Macbeth. It is also the most sickening of a series of events that loses him the support of the thanes.

Quiz

Can you explain the prophecies?

Macbeth receives six prophecies from the Witches in the course of the play. Can you explain what happens as a result of each?

a) In Act 1, Scene 3, the Witches hail Macbeth as Thane of Cawdor. Why is he surprised? How does he find out that they are right?

b) What does the letter to Lady Macbeth (1.5) show about Macbeth's reaction to the prophecy that he will be 'King hereafter'?

c) How does the warning to 'beware Macduff' come true?

d) Why is the assurance that 'no man born of woman' can harm him deceptive?

e) How does the prophecy about Birnam Wood and Dunsinane come true?

f) Is there any proof that Banquo's descendants did become Kings of Scotland?

Can you compare the scenes?

See what comparisons you can make between this scene and the Witches' other major appearances in Act 1, Scenes 1 and 3.

a) Give examples from both scenes of references to the Witches' familiars (animal demons who attend on witches).

b) Find lines which suggest that the Witches are dancing or moving in a ring to create their charms.

c) How do they know that Macbeth is about to arrive?

d) What similarities do you find in the way they speak to Macbeth in both scenes?

e) How do the Witches leave Macbeth?

Do you know these words?

Do you know the meaning of these words, all used in Act 4, Scene 1?

a) 'bodements' (line 95)

b) 'howlet' (line 17)

c) 'firstlings' (line 146)

d) 'sceptres' (line 120)

e) 'lion-mettled' (line 89)

f) 'harped' (line 73)

g) 'germens' (line 58)

h) 'yeasty' or 'yesty' (line 52)

i) 'ravined' (line 24)

j) 'flighty' (line 144)

Sample question

There are several points in the play where supernatural events are important, but in this scene the Witches and their spell, and their effect on Macbeth, are particularly significant. Explain how Shakespeare creates a strong impression of their evil nature. You might want to include:

- *the way the Witches speak;*
- *the influence they have on Macbeth;*
- *the importance of their prophecies.*

In your introduction, talk about some of the other supernatural events in the play – the ghost of Banquo and the dagger that leads to Duncan, for example. You need not go into detail, but showing that you know about them means you have a wider knowledge of the play.

The first part of the scene does not add anything to the story, but it does help the audience form an opinion of the Witches. Mention the unpleasant nature of some of the things they use to make their spell, but don't go through the whole list. More importantly, look at the way they talk, which is intended to sound very unnatural. This is partly because they speak in rhyming couplets and partly because they use shorter lines than the usual iambic pentameter, which gives it a very strong sense of rhythm. It is also very repetitive. Why do you think Shakespeare aims to create this effect before Macbeth even enters?

To explain the effect the Witches have on Macbeth, you will need to look at the events that have already happened. They have already given him one set of prophecies, all of which have come true. Macbeth knows he is in a dangerous position. He no longer trusts anybody, but instead relies more and more on what the Witches tell him. Describe the mood he is in when he first enters the scene. Look at the way he speaks to them: 'How now, you secret, black and midnight hags!' (line 47). Which phrases suggest he is demanding and insistent? As the new prophecies are revealed, Macbeth goes through several mood changes: 'thou hast harped my fear aright' (line 73), 'Sweet bodements! Good!' (line 95). What other examples can you find?

The prophecies are important because he relies on them to give him extra strength. They tell him he has nothing to fear until a wood uproots itself and walks to his castle. Explain how this apparently impossible prediction comes true. How does it affect Macbeth when it does? Explain the other predictions in the same way.

In your conclusion, talk about what you think is the most evil part of this scene. Is it the witches' spell? Macbeth's threat to kill Macduff? The apparitions? Why do you think so?

Quiz

ANSWERS

ACT 1, SCENE 1

Can you fill in the background?

a) Norway. Sweno.

b) Macdonwald.

c) 'kerns and gallowglasses' (footsoldiers and Irish levies) from the Western Isles.

d) Cawdor. He is stripped of his title and immediately executed.

e) King Sweno. Macbeth. Malcolm.

Can you trace the plot?

a) He decides to stay with Macbeth whom he trusts completely.

b) After killing Duncan he decides to kill Banquo and his son to make the throne safe.

c) He calls her his 'dearest partner of greatness': he intends to be King.

d) By Lady Macbeth's encouragement and insults and her organisation of Duncan's murder.

e) (i) Both lead him to evil. (ii) The later ones are deceptive in a way that these are not. The references to 'no man born of woman' and Birnam Wood mislead Macbeth about events.

Do you know these words?

a) successful or flourishing

b) bodily (i.e. solid)

c) benefit

d) strained

e) imaginary

f) a term of abuse, probably meaning 'witch' or 'foul-mouthed woman'

g) tempting/encouraging

h) lean-to shed

i) meantime

j) speculation (wondering what will happen)

ACT 1, SCENES 5–7

Can you trace the characters?

a) Malcolm decides to go to England, Donalbain to Ireland (Act 2, Scene 3). They are blamed for planning their father's murder. Macduff reports this in Act 2, Scene 4, lines 24–27.

b) He enlists the aid of the King of England in preparing an army under Seyward (or Siward); he enlists the assistance of Macduff; he links with an army of dissatisfied Scots and defeats Macbeth.

c) He knows too much about the Witches, but, more importantly, his descendants will be kings, so he might attack Macbeth. In Act 3 Macbeth arranges the murders of Banquo (who dies) and his son, Fleance (who escapes).

d) Angus and Lennox finally appear in the Scots rebel army in Act 5, Ross with the English army, having gone to England in Act 4, Scene 3. Ross and Lennox are part of Macbeth's court (3.4) and Lennox co-operates with Macbeth in Act 4, Scene 1, but there are signs of their opposition to Macbeth, especially Lennox in Act 3, Scene 6 and Ross in Act 4, Scene 2.

e) He is not going to the coronation and fears he will not fit in with the new regime (lines 37-38).

f) By killing his family (4.2).

g) As a man not 'of woman born' he kills Macbeth.

Can you tell what happens next?

a) (i) There are signs of it in Act 2, in his fears over killing Duncan, but it rapidly decreases through the play. (ii) In Act 3 he arranges murders without help from Lady Macbeth. (iii) By Act 4 he has turned to killing innocent women and children.

b) In Act 2 totally. The strain, however, produces her mental breakdown.

c) Duncan must be looked after as a King. Lady Macbeth proves the perfect hostess (e.g. 2.1, lines 12–16). He must also be killed and she organises that as well.

d) Yes; she also drugs them (2.2, lines 6–8).

Do you know these words?

a) a flask for chemical experiments

b) proverb

c) hanging

d) supernatural

e) deceive

f) giving birth

g) end

h) feasting and merry-making

i) murkiest

j) corner

ACT 2, SCENES 2–3

Can you trace the character?

The quotations given below, all good answers, are examples. They are not always the only answers.

a) 'Two truths are told/As happy prologues to the swelling Act/Of the imperial theme' (lines 126–128). 'Present fears/Are less than horrible imaginings.' (lines 136–137)

b) 'Yet do I fear thy nature:/It is too full o'the milk of human-kindness/To catch the nearest way.' (lines 14–16)

c) 'It is the bloody business which informs/Thus to mine eyes.' (lines 48–49)

d) 'Wake Duncan with thy knocking. I would thou couldst.' (line 74)

e) 'Be innocent of the knowledge, dearest chuck,/Till thou applaud the deed.' (lines 45–46)

f) 'I am in blood/Stepped in so far, that, should I wade no more,/Returning were as tedious as go o'er.' (lines 135–137)

g) The 'tomorrow and tomorrow and tomorrow' speech (lines 19–28).

Can you explain the image?

a) 'Gild' means 'paint'. 'Gilding' their faces will make it look as if the grooms are 'guilty'.

b) The first use of 'blood' is indicating closeness of family (in this case, the Royal Family, line 95 uses 'blood' in the same way). 'Bloody' refers to shedding blood: they might be murdered.

c) To make Duncan seem holy. Kings were anointed with holy oil at their coronations.

d) The second course is the main course, so sleep is the main thing that sustains life.

Do you know these words?

a) having eaten and drunk too much

b) many

c) small crevice

d) a mythical creature whose look turned people to stone

e) fire (lightning?)

f) skein, as of silk or wool. Some editions prefer the spelling 'sleeve', with its usual meaning.

g) secret, not revealed

h) treats with medicine

i) hot drinks

j) meet/talk

ACT 3, SCENE 4

Can you trace the character?

a) He is not evil enough. 'Art not without ambition, but without/The illness (evil) should attend it.' (1.5, lines 17–18). Too much human kindness and too much honesty are also good answers.

b) She entertains Duncan and his party; she drugs the guards; she returns the daggers. She also, of course, persuades Macbeth to go through with it.

c) She faints (2.3, line 115).

d) None. Macbeth even says he wants her to be 'innocent of the knowledge'.

e) 'A little water clears us of this deed' (line 67).

Can you find the image?

a) serpent (line 28). The serpent (snake) represents poison and danger.

b) blood (line 135). Blood as guilt is an image that occurs very often in this scene and elsewhere.

c) sleep (line 140). Sleep suggests innocence and peace and Macbeth has lacked it since the murder of Duncan.

d) fit (line 54). This is Macbeth's second 'fit' in this scene: these fits and fevers show how guilt and fear are destroying him.

e) man (line 57). Lady Macbeth's questioning of Macbeth's manhood (courage) goes back to Act 1.

Do you know these words?

a) made white

b) magpies and small crows, used in sacrifices to predict the future

c) the best beyond compare

d) stomachs

e) from the Anglo-Saxon 'Wyrd' meaning 'fate'; the Witches have power over our fate.

f) first, like a beginner

g) bone-houses

h) imprisoned (all four words in the list mean much the same)

i) deeply cut

j) under one roof

ACT 4, SCENE 1

Can you explain the prophecies?

a) He thinks the Thane is alive, 'a prosperous gentleman'. Ross and Angus soon bring the news that Cawdor is a traitor and Macbeth has been given the title.

b) He is already brooding on 'greatness': he hopes to be king.

c) Macduff helps to lead Malcolm's army and kills Macbeth.

d) Because Macduff was not born in the orthodox way, but prematurely by surgery (5.6, lines 53-55)

e) Malcolm's troops conceal themselves behind branches from the wood as they approach Dunsinane.

f) Not really, but the audiences would have recognised the 'two-fold balls and treble sceptres', reference to James VI of Scotland/I of England, as evidence.

Can you compare the scenes?

a) Greymalkin and Paddock (1.1, line 8); the cat, the hedge-pig and Harpier (4.1, lines 1–3)

b) 'The Weird Sisters, hand in hand...' (1.3, lines 31–35) and the 'Double, double...' refrain (4.1, lines 10–11, etc.)

c) By the sound of a drum (1.3, line 29) and 'by the pricking of my thumbs' (4.1, line 44). They recognise him as 'something wicked'.

d) The echo effect ('Hail', 'Hail', 'Hail' or 'Speak', 'Demand', 'We'll answer') is the most obvious similarity.

e) They suddenly vanish, no one knows where to.

Do you know these words?

a) predictions

b) owlet, a small owl, possibly a young one

c) first ideas

d) ornamental rods, part of Royal regalia

e) with the temper of a lion

f) guessed

g) germs, seeds

h) frothy

i) glutted, over-full

j) swift